Haiku Dreams

A personal haiku journal with images and commentary

Jason Hanrahan

Dedication

This book is dedicated to Aisha Yusaf and Allan John Viljoen who inspired and encouraged my haiku writing.

You only have yourselves to blame ;o)

Table of Contents

Introduction

Foreword

I have to confess that for much of my time on this rotating rock in space, the art of haiku had largely passed me by. Poetry (and a great deal of art) I would mostly dismiss as pretentious nonsense (or often something less polite!!!) I vaguely remember covering haiku in haste in school perhaps aged about 12 years old, but little more. More recently a friend who is a fabulous baker and photographer would enhance her mouth-wateringly gorgeous images of buns, cakes and cookies lightly dusted with icing sugar on Facebook with deep and meaningful haiku verses. My interest was piqued.

I have always had a fascination for Japanese culture, initially as a result of the influence of manga and anime, but later through a growing interest in bonsai and koi keeping. This introduced me to phrases such as "wabi-sabi" and Zen. I am also a voracious reader, and often read over a hundred books each year, and my attention has recently turned to Japanese literature, Zen writings and the Japanese classics. Recently this has covered **The Tale of Genji**, **Travels with a Writing Brush, One Hundred Poets, One Poem Each**, **Zen Fool Ryokan** and **Essays in Idleness** amongst others. It was only a matter of time before I would find myself absorbing the works of haiku masters such as Buson, Basho, Issa and Ryokan. With their beautifully poetic sense of transient beauty, something inside me was awakened.

For me, a haiku represents a snapshot in time, a vignette perfectly captured in minimalistic language. It conjures a vivid image and evokes an emotive response. Similarly, a beautiful image or photograph can tell a powerful story through lighting, framing and composition. Indeed, a picture paints a thousand words. It seemed natural to combine the two to generate a powerful reaction. The limitations of the form also appeal to me as an intellectual challenge, a word game used to demonstrate wit and wisdom. It is playful. It is joyous.

Amongst my reading were also books on happiness, and a key learning was simply finding things to be grateful for. Some suggested writing a list every day, or telling people how much you appreciate them. To be thankful for the beauty around us, for the small things that we might otherwise miss in the rush of our busy lives. Out of this sentiment sprang my haiku journal, a tattered notebook where I scribble my thoughts. Strictly speaking it includes not only haiku in the classic sense, but also senryu – like haiku but a more satirical commentary on people, politics, society.

The haiku included here are the direct results of a conscious effort to be more mindful and Zen, to appreciate wabi sabi and the beauty and impermanence of the little things, to be thankful every day. They were written during 2020, a year much marred by the worldwide Covid-19 pandemic, as will be evident from several of the verses. My partner has often had to patiently stand by as I pause in the middle of a country walk to compose a verse and check it's syllable count on my mobile phone or as I took a photo to accompany it. I don't claim to be a great poet, but on the principle that if you throw enough stuff at the wall some of it may stick, I simply wrote and wrote and wrote. In the middle of work, whilst commuting, in the dark hours in the middle of the night when I couldn't sleep, or the stillness of the morning listening to the dawn chorus. Whenever inspiration struck, I recorded my thoughts in my haiku journal.

Composing these haiku and senryu gave me great personal pleasure and satisfaction, as did matching them with evocative images and I hope that some of that can be imparted to you as reader.

I humbly thank you for taking time to indulge me, and to read this work. May you too find reason to be thankful every day.

Jason Hanrahan
November 2021.

On Form and Format

My views on the "correct" format for haiku, and whether the strict definition should be followed change from day to day, and depending which side of the bed I get out of.

For the most part I try to follow the 5-7-5 syllable format, over three lines of verse. To me this requires some skill or effort in order to wrangle your thoughts within the construct, and can lead to playfulness and creative thinking. This is what the art of haiku is about. On the other hand, the formal requirements should not strangle out the spirit of creativity, and the following of formal rules can lead to artificial constructs or an obligation to insert unnecessary words and filler.

As with many forms of art, including bonsai, I would suggest that the rules should be treated as guidelines only – and that you are free to break those prescriptive rules – but you should do so only consciously and in full awareness of what you are doing and why. By way of example several of the verses in this collection are deliberately in a 6-6-6 format. It amused me no end to adopt this for verses about a certain politician… suggestive of a hellish connection.

Some of the haiku here would be properly considered by purists to be senryu. A senryu lacks the seasonal "kigo" word or reference, and is typically more concerned with a satirical or humorous view or observation.

I also agonised at length over the format to adopt when presenting the haiku. Should I simply publish my verses in strict chronological order, with no supplementary material? In this way the reader could bring their own imagination and interpretation to bear. Or should I include explanatory notes?

My final decision to include commentary and images came after reading a number of works like **The Narrow Road to Deep North** by Matsuo Basho and **The Life and Zen Haiku Poetry of Santoka Taneda**. Knowing the setting, context or thought processes that inspired the verse might enlighten others looking to write their own haiku, or provide a richer insight into the writer's intended meaning of the verse.

The images similarly have their own visual poetry. Like a haiku, a photograph is brief snapshot in time and can capture mood and essence. Many of the images were the inspiration for the accompanying verses, or taken at the time the verse was composed.
I hope that you will agree with this decision and enjoy the resulting collection.

About The Images

All images were taken by the author using the camera on an iPhone 11 and processed through an image processing application called Insta Toon to create the consistent, stylised look.

The Haiku

Zen Verses

Koi splash playfully
A buddha sits serenely
In the dappled shade

A Buddha beneath
A towering banana tree
Just like Basho?

The classical 17th century Japanese haiku poet and Buddhist Basho got his name from the banana tree that was gifted to him by his students, and which he planted next to his ramshackle hut. In my conservatory I noticed that quite by accident I have a Buddha statue which is sat beneath a banana tree.

By a glassy lake
I sit in contemplation
Still waters run deep

By a copse of trees
He meditates serenely
Chromatic buddha

At the Yorkshire Sculpture Park there is an installation in the upper park of a multi coloured Buddha figure with one eye, covered in mosaic tiles.

Waves ceaselessly wash
Over a white shingle beach
Worries come and go

Life's worries are apt to be like the waves washing up a beach. The tide comes in. The tide goes out. What might seem terrible today, may soon be forgotten, replaced by newer concerns. We need to learn to let go, particularly those things which we cannot control.

Leaf falls in the woods
Is it very like the sound
Of one hand clapping?

A Zen koan is a thought puzzle or impossible riddle to which there is no correct answer. Here I am playfully mashing together ideas of Zen koans such as "What is the sound of one hand clapping?" and sayings such as "If there is no-one there to hear it, does a tree make any noise when it falls in the forest?"

Soft wind stirred chimes
Gentle music of the spheres -
Sings to my essence

Radiant sunlight
In a shimmering raindrop -
Rainbow colour wash

My green tea whisk stand:
Sleeks, shiny, jade ceramic
Looks like a butt plug

According to an authority on the subject, they have a similar shape.

Purple pagoda
Temple to nature's beauty
I pay my respects

In my garden I admired a beautiful flower with cascading bell flowers
that resembled a multi-tiered temple.

They slumber soundly
So untroubled by life's woes
Simple, honest stones

As the Buddha said
Attachments bring such sorrow
Same true of email

This boiling lobster
By formal Buddhist teachings
Could be my grandma

Life's balancing act
When fickle fate hands you rocks
Why not make rock stacks

So the saying goes "when life hands you lemons, make lemonade".
I imagined life handing out rocks, and people making dramatic,
artistic rock stacks instead. Unexpected, and exciting.

Biting mosquito
In a previous life may
Have been my mother

In some Buddhist teachings we accumulate karma through our lives
which dictates how we will be re-incarnated. To Buddhists all life is
sacred, and the verse here is suggesting that by killing the mosquito

you may in fact by killing your former relative.

Cherry Blossom

Cherry blossom stirs
Dappled light on mossy stone
Too transient beauty

I was particularly mesmerised watching the light and shade moving over a mossy wall as a light breeze stirred the leaves and blossom of the cherry tree. The cherry blossom, though beautiful, is celebrated because it's splendour is also so very short lived.

My heart sings to see
Long forgotten friends returned
First cherry blossom

Absorbed in his work
Too occupied with blossom
To acknowledge me

A bee is busy searching for pollen and seems blissfully unaware or unconcerned with my presence.

Delicate petals
Stirred by a chilling breeze
Pink winter cherry

Soft pink confetti
Falling to the grass beneath
The old cherry tree

At the death of spring
Walking on a carpet of
Pink cherry blossom

Life Lessons

Sometimes it feels like
The path you're on is uphill
In both directions

Naturally the joke is that if you go up a hill, then you must come down. Sometimes life is not quite like that.

Source of my troubles
All the problems I can see
And ones I cannot

Another tongue in cheek verse which covers all the possibilities for trouble.

The surface serene
Many struggles go unseen
Reflecting real life

This verse was inspired by watching a swan paddling on a still lake. We see the still and graceful swan above, but not the furiously paddling feet beneath.

Quite often people suffer in silence and what we see on the surface belies the struggle or effort required underneath. That gift you received ungraciously may have been paid for with the last remaining money or the meal you slighted with a throwaway remark may have taken hours of careful preparation. The person giving the strong and powerful presentation may be falling apart inside due to grief or the ending of a relationship. We need to learn to see beyond the façade, to be more appreciative, and kinder, and wiser to others.

Stately Homes and Gardens

I am fortunate enough to be a member of both English Heritage and the National Trust, who manage and restore historical, heritage properties, gardens and estates in England. There are many important historical houses which tell the story of the making of our country.

But many of them also harbour a darker past, with family fortunes made in slavery and human misery.

Brodsworth Hall, near Doncaster is one such property. Family home to the Thellussons, this is one of the most complete examples of a Victorian country house in England. Typical of such a property are the expansive, landscaped grounds and the carefully manicured gardens. These were huge vanity works, showcasing the conspicuous wealth and influence of the owners. Like many such properties the family wealth derived from, amongst other things, investments in slaving and plantation work.

> Ionic temple
> So much more money than sense

Vanity project

Dark windows like eyes
Staring from a brooding hall
Haunted by it's past

This could relate to any one of a number of old buildings and ruins owned or managed by either English Heritage or the National Trust. In fact it was written whilst staying at Dunsley Hall, a charming and characterful country hotel near Whitby, North Yorkshire.

Work in the Garden

Having previously dug out a koi pond in the garden, our lockdown project was to transform one corner into a Japanese styled rock/tea garden. It involved shifting crates of rock, sacks of gravel, and days of painting and constructing the gazebo. It is now a suitable haven for relaxing, contemplating the nature of everything and composing haiku.

Grey jumble of rock
Is a Japanese garden
It won't build itself

This jumble of wood
Is a Japanese tea house
It won't build itself

Paint paint paint paint paint
Paint paint paint paint paint paint paint
Paint paint paint paint done

I like that this one playfully highlights the monotony and then the surprise and sense of relief when the job is actually complete. At the time it did seem endless.

When the work is done
Time to enjoy peace and rest
In the Zen garden

Finally, job done, it is time to eventually enjoy the fruits of our labours, domestic arguments and depleted bank balance.

The Beauty and Majesty of Trees

Trees have existed in one form or another for 350 million years and well before the advent of man. They outnumber us 422 to 1. They are incredible, majestic beings that live their lives at a different pace from us, and far outlive our short lifespans. Recent scientific knowledge shows that they live in communities and can communicate and support each other through underground networks of symbiotic mycorrhiza fungus. Long before the last tree could ever be cut down the damage to the atmosphere would have wiped out humanity. I believe that trees will be here long after we have gone extinct. The Earth is not ours. It is theirs.

They were here before
And will endure long after
The Earth is theirs. Trees

Over Summer my neighbour hired someone to cut back her overgrown trees. I hope she didn't pay them too much! I wasn't entirely happy with this verse so had a couple of attempts, shifting words around.

Dead branch amid green
My neighbour hired
Tree butchers not surgeons

Dead branch amid green
My neighbour seems to have hired
Butchers not surgeons

Mental note: An enthusiastic eighteen year old with a chainsaw is NOT a tree surgeon.

In my mind there is a poetic hierarchy of trees. Oak trees are the masculine, aged kings. The silver birch is the elegant, regal queen, with her weeping branches, striking white bark with black darts and fissures. The Japanese maple, by comparison, is the delicate, showy princess. These are themes which recur throughout my tree related haiku.

Majestic tree boughs
Leaves dangling in the warm breeze
Robbed of your beauty

Leaning on his stick
Bears the weight of aged limbs
Gnarly old oak tree

In the grounds of Nostell Priory, near Wakefield, there is an old oak tree with a low horizontal branch which is supported by a sturdy wooden prop. This made me think of an elderly gent supporting himself on his walking stick.

Beneath red maples
Dappled sunlight dancing on
Verdant velvet moss

Earth bound tentacles

Life sustaining mossy limbs
Ancient tree roots

Skeletal fingers
Clawing at leaden grey sky
Rotting tree remains

An old man stooping
Four centuries he has stood
Venerable oak

Clinging on for life
Exposed limbs grasping at rock
Twisted cliff top tree

Skeletal tree forms
Silhouettes against grey skies
Steady cold rain falls

Between bare branches
Lacy cobwebs hung with dew
Catch blazing sunlight

Blazing larch tree leaves
Against the dark bare woodland
Fiery autumn gold

Larch trees are the only deciduous conifer. Their needles turn a spectacular yellow-gold before dropping in late autumn.

Against cold grey skies
A tracery of fine branches
A lone crow laments

Corner of a park
She weeps deeply for spring
Leafless silver birch

The birch has a natural weeping growth habit. I like the dual meaning here.

In her finery
She refuses to sleep
Japanese maple

Sat amid the snows
A flushed pink princess blushes
Maple still in leaf

Japanese maples will often put on a blazing show of colour in autumn, turning spectacular reds, pinks and oranges before losing their leaves. This particular tree held onto it's leaves especially late into the year.

Climbing from the soil
Like a huge splayed octopus
Gnarly grey tree roots

Does he feel the cold
This writhing twisted old man
An ancient oak tree

Slender white beauty
Stands amid the frozen snows
Regal silver birch

See her resting now
Her eighty year reign over
Fallen silver birch

By tree standards the silver birch is relatively short lived at 80-140 years. By contrast oak trees can live beyond 400 years and the yew tree can exceed 1000 years.

They huddle for warmth
Tender kissing silver trunks
Even trees know love

This verse was inspired on a woodland walk when I saw two silver birch trees growing together, their trunks entwined, as though in an embrace.

They gently caress
The lapping, cooling waters
Weeping willow leaves

No cream or cure
Will revive her faded beauty
Ruptured old birch bark

As they age, the striking white bark of the silver birch tree develops
dark diamond shaped fissures, looking like darts cut into fabric.

Silver and diamonds
Adorn their finest garments
Majestic birch trees

The Sea

There is something incredibly primal about the sea and our relationship to it. Perhaps we have an inbuilt genetic memory that link us to it through our ancestors who first flopped and crawled out of the waters. The sound of the sea lapping, washing and rolling over the sands is intensely hypnotic, and the sight of waves swelling and crashing against the rocks reminds of it's immense power. No wonder then that it has inspired poetic visions and haiku.

Sea spray splashed rock
White caps on roiling grey waves
A lonely gull cries

These following verses were inspired by watching the sun rise at the picturesque 18th century village and port at Charlestown on the south coast of Cornwall, UK.

Yellow sun ascends
On ceaseless rolling water
A sunrise at sea

The sun greets the day
Waves wash gently over sand
Tall ship at anchor

A cloud enveiled sun
Kisses undulating waves
A new day begins

Further round the coast, the beautiful bay of St Ives, much revered by artists for it's fantastic light was totally hidden from view by a sea fret (sea mist).

Thick sea mist conceals
A stunning scenic view
Bay of St Ives

So, ironically, I am looking at the beautiful scenery, but cannot actually see it.

Undulating glints
Golden sunlight garnished waves
Gulls soaring above

There is something magical about the way sunlight glints and reflects off the water.

A sea breeze stirring
Lifting crying gulls aloft
Above the grey waves

A lonely light house
Bastion against the dark
Shining beacon home

Cooking and Baking

During lockdown many people took the opportunity to learn new skills. For some that was learning languages, or taking up some artistic hobby. For me it was to rediscover baking, though not all my delicious (in my opinion) efforts were fully appreciated.

> Recipe abused,
> Chocolate muffins sunken
> Partner unimpressed

Claiming that someone cooks "just like my mother used to" is usually intended to be a compliment. However, I wondered, what if you were unfortunate enough to have a mother who couldn't cook? It was an opportunity for humour, too good to miss.

> Just like my mother's:
> A cake baked with love
> Burnt, inedible

Sea Mist

Through the drifting mists
Hopeful holiday makers
Searching for sun beams

On a visit to Redcar on the East coast of England the sea was obscured from sight by a thick, drifting sea mist. Despite this there were tourists sat out on the beach. To the North an industrial plant on the seafront was occasionally visible through the drifting vapour, and gave the whole scene a surreal, post apocalyptic look which inspired the verse above.

A Miscellany of Verse

I live close to the Yorkshire Sculpture Park. In the grounds of the park this sinister, otherworldly structure is hidden amongst a copse of silver birch trees. It looks like some fearful Lovecraftian ancient temple or perhaps an alien spacecraft which long since crashed into the Earth, just like in Stephen King's tale **The Tommyknockers**..

> Fearful geometry
> Amid the trees darkly squats
> Mossy pyramid

> Big Issue seller
> Gives the world a toothy grin

A smile costs nothing
I am struck here by how the smallest gestures, which cost us
nothing, can have incredible value.

I have long since developed a habit that when I see a Big Issue
seller I give them all my loose change, no matter how much that
might be. However, in more recent times, with the advent of
cashless society, I tend to carry only my bank card. Not all change
is positive.

Swiftly beating heart
Within a mass of feathers
Fly free little bird

Cotton candy clouds
Float in a silver blue sky
Moisture on the breeze

Concrete Human zoo
Young Offenders Institute
Don't feed the animals

Brain freeze not likely
When eating frozen ice cream
If you have no brain

It is not something which I have ever personally experienced, but
my partner occasionally suffers "brain freeze" when eating ice
cream. I teased that a brain was pre-requisite for that to be possible.

He vents his spleen
This is quite an achievement
Thanks to the transplant

This was an intentionally nonsense verse, amusingly playing on the
idea that someone who is recovering from a critical organ transplant
might be "venting his spleen" by arguing furiously with someone.
This is a miracle considering he was previously imminently staring
death in the face.

Burning sensation

Painful stinging when passing water
Seems you're in trouble

This rather puerile play on the word "urine" amused me endlessly.
On the down side, it felt like I was pissing boiling acid.

Is it uniform
Grubby grey, unwashed sweat pants
Underemployed youth

People who stand at the top of escalators, or blocking shop
doorways gossiping endlessly infuriate me. How can people be so
totally unaware that there are other people around and they are
causing an obstruction?

You cannot stand there
Oblivious to others
Causing obstruction

Alarming to see
When the power goes off
How many don't know the code

After a recent spate of power cuts all the burglar alarms on the
surrounding houses were sounding for an uncomfortably long time. I
could only conclude that the owners either did not know the code to
switch them off, or could not easily find them.

Sat gathering dust
Unused gym apparatus
Convenient clothes horse

Every year enthusiastic people, fired with New Year's resolutions,
enrol at gyms or start an exercise regime, only to give up very
shortly after. And it seems everyone I know who has ever owned
home gym equipment ends up using it to hang clothing on. Myself
included.

My Facebook timeline keeps getting hit by adverts for high end
fashions like Prada:

What a sight they make
These preening prancing peacocks
Models without pants

In this particular advertising campaign the pasty models were dressed for the beach in "flasher mac" raincoats, what looked like Nazi stormtrooper helmets and brogues. However, they seem to have forgotten to put their trousers on. In one image, the guy standing in the sea appeared to have neglected to take his shoes off. Tragic.

A petulant child
Cries with sad howls of anguish
This, my neighbour's dog

I have always believed that dogs are like sometimes petulant, always overly enthusiastic children. They are so full of energy and excitement that every day spent with you, every walk, every day trip out is a new exciting adventure. Every moment is the "best ever". Until the next moment.

"Are you coming now?"
Question asked in urgency
"Momentarily"

A lioness roar
Tiny woman in black robes
Ruth Bader Ginsberg

This is my tribute to an American lawyer and jurist who served as an associate justice of the Supreme Court of the United States until her death just before the Presidential election in 2020. Despite her tiny stature, she had significant impact and influence.

"It's coming home"
A pigs bladder kickabout
Tribal politics

Almost forgotten
In a tangled knot of trees
Dark stone obelisk

Walking through the parkland and lakeside walk at The Yorkshire Sculpture Park we were surprised to come across this stone obelisk, partly obscured by weeds and tangled foliage in the woodland.

Gold coins free to all
At the end of the rainbow
Kill a leprechaun

According to folklore, if you find the end of the rainbow you will uncover a pot of gold. The unspoken problem though, is that the leprechaun guarding it is unlikely to give it up without a fight.

In a crowded room
Taking nervous sips of wine
Rather than engage

This one was prompted by social anxiety that comes from being in a room full of strangers. It is far easier to befriend your drink and use it as a shield rather than engage with actual human beings.

Newly seeking work
Will consider anything
Excepting real work

Call me Frankenstein
New life contrived in a tank
Hello Sea Monkeys

I felt like Dr Frankenstein after breeding new life in a tank of "sea monkeys", aka artemia brine shrimps.

They whirl and cavort
In a droplet of water
Microscopic beasts

Ash rains from the sky
Grazed knuckles covered with blood
Each has a story

Soft blue mist curling

Drifting through dense foliage
Aroma of fire

Mister Mouse

From time to time my cats will bring in a mousey offering from the garden which puts up a spirited fight and makes for the shelter of the nearest piece of furniture. I know when I come down to breakfast and they have set up an intense vigil by a chair that there is probably a live mouse hiding underneath that will need liberating. In this case the mouse took up refuge behind the fire place.

> Hey there mister mouse
> Hiding under the fireplace
> Don't burn your whiskers

The picture is a dramatic reconstruction.

Other gifts have included birds, a rat, several earth worms, frequent frogs and numerous mice (or their chewed remnants). I have absolutely no idea how they managed it, but they also brought in three bats.

A Walk in the Woods

Since the 1980s the Japanese have practiced "shinrin-yoku" or "forest bathing" where they encourage people to spend time outdoors, amongst the trees, bathed in and absorbing the calming natural ambiance. It is believed to significantly mitigate the root cause of a multitude of ailments, namely stress. Excess stress can contribute to headaches, high blood pressure, heart problems, among many other illnesses and health problems.

I am fortunate in that I live in the suburbs, between town and country, and within only a short time I can be amongst the local fields and woodland. The beauty of nature is always a rich source of inspiration for haiku and an opportunity to enjoy and appreciate the wonders of the natural world. In woodland, I am always particularly struck by the way light shifts and dances as it shines through the gently swaying branches and leaves overhead.

Dappled canopy
Questing beams of sunlight
Probe the forest floor

Dappled canopy
A probing beam of sunlight
Strobes the forest floor

In a leafy glade
Bright red agaric mushrooms
Fairy parasols

Fly agaric mushrooms grow amid the dead leaves of birch trees and are the picturesque red capped mushrooms with white spots and stems of fairytales. They are also poisonous.

A trilling thrush sits
Amid red rowan berries
Swoops low and is gone

On a country walk
It saddens my heart to see
Dog poo tree in fruit

Of course the "dog poo tree" is just any tree strewn with discarded bags of dog poo, and the fruit are the hanging bags caught in the branches. Like Broken Windows theory, first studied by Philip Zimbardo, it seems that as soon as one person has thrown their parcel of dog excrement into the trees, it gives tacit permission for others to follow their example.

Rain

Rods of cold rain fall
Heavy from a leaden sky
Coffee warms my hands

Here I was safely sat indoors in the warmth, with a hot mug of coffee, while the rain fell heavily outside, cold rivulets running down the window.

After the rain falls
Lightening skies, renewed hope
The grass still wet though

There is hope that after the rain better times will return. Life's troubles are apt to be like that.

> A cold, driving rain
> Lashes down, stinging my eyes
> Is the sky crying

Sometimes I like to consider the same idea from a different viewpoint, what if it is not the sky crying? The denial here seems overstated – methinks the writer doth protest too much. The rain is just a convenient excuse.

> A cold, driving rain
> Lashes down, stinging my eyes
> I am not crying

> A cool grey zephyr
> Carries moisture in the air
> Reflects my grey mood

> Leaden skies threaten
> Rumours of rumbling thunder
> Moisture on the breeze

> Leaden skies threaten
> Rumours of rumbling thunder
> Tension in the air

Although ostensibly about a brewing storm, these last two were actually written after witnessing the unusual sight of a Boeing Chinhook tandem rotor helicopter passing overhead. The sound was quite ominous and it's presence perhaps a sinister portent.

Religion

> The trouble I've seen
> Nobody knows but Jesus
> Not entirely true

As is often the case, this verse came to me after having the words of the song "Nobody Knows The Trouble I've Seen" lodged in my head like an ear worm. I could only exorcise it by composing this wry verse. It should be noted that I am not personally religious.

> It can move mountains
> Or fly planes into buildings
> Faith works such wonders

The same strongly held beliefs that can perform miracles can also just as easily result in acts of barbarity. Hence this take on the idea that faith can move mountains. It was the French Enlightenment writer and philosopher Voltaire who famously said that "Those who can make you believe absurdities, can make you commit atrocities."

It's a foolish thing
To revere any mortal
As purely divine

The same is true in any field, not just religion.

Keeps them all awake
Palindromic theorists
This: Do geese see god?

A palindrome being a word or phrase which reads the same forwards as backwards, this one appealed to my twisted sense of humour.

They watch me pissing
Mother and child spying on
My private moments

If on the face of it this sounds weird and offensive then please don't worry. It's actually about the picture of the Madonna and Child which was bought for me as a house warming gift, and which hangs in my downstairs toilet. Since I'm from good Irish Catholic stock, I am least feel a ghost of a twinge of guilt about writing this one.

The Countryside

Corner of a field
Walls defying gravity
A ramshackle hut

Get a load of that
Fresh country air fills your lungs
Smells of cow manure

There is an old sketch by British comedian Lenny Henry where he is strolling down a country lane, breathing in huge gasps of air, beside a field of gently lowing cows. "Get a load of that fresh country air." Dramatic pause. "Bloody horrible isn't it". Although it must now be perhaps 35 years old it stuck in my memory, and I wanted to capture the essence of it in this haiku.

Ankle deep in mud
I climb this hill on my knees
And down on my arse

The dangers of country walks in autumn when everything is bogged down in mud and perilously slippery.

Onwards ever up
Legs tremble under dark boughs

Summit - heart attack!!!
That feeling when you finally reach the top, but you are bent double gasping for breath... This one came after a steep climb from a valley floor in Dalby Forest, to see the Bridestones, a collection of dramatic formations made of Jurassic sedimentary rock deposited on top of the hills 150 million years ago.

In the Lake District clouds drifted and whisped across the faces of the hills and mountain sides. I imagined the mountains to be immense, immoveable sleeping giants, their heads in the clouds and their feet firmly planted in the earth.

> White cloud drifts over
> A dark and sombre mountain
> A still lake reflects
>
> Looming out the mist
> Dark, pine tree covered mountains
> White sheep bathed in dew
>
> Heads amongst the clouds
> With feet planted on firm ground
> Vast dreaming mountains
>
> Mist shrouded mountains
> Filling grey horizons, dream
> For eternity

On the moors of Dartmoor in Cornwall, thick drifting mists came and went frequently obscuring the view across the bleak moorlands, giving the place a haunted, otherworldly atmosphere. We were fortunate enough to visit between COVID lockdowns in the UK, and just before the second wave swept across the country. We should have been on a luxury two week cruise around the Canary Islands.

> Passing through Dartmoor
> They shoot horses don't they?
> We all have to eat

As is often the case, some phrase or term which becomes lodged in my head becomes the seed of inspiration. It can be a saying, nursery rhyme, a quote from a film, or sometimes a song lyric. Although I have never seen it, there is a film called They Shoot Horses, Don't They? It came to mind while travelling across the moors, famed for its population of wild horses. Although horse meat is commonly eaten elsewhere, the idea repulses British sensibilities.

Livestock grazing in
A patchwork of green and brown
Cool rain drifts across

Rolling cloud obscures
Where cows and sheep stand grazing
Damp and verdant fields

Tendrils drift across
White, creeping, living, breathing
Cornish moorland mist

The drifting moorland mists became a common feature of our trip to Cornwall. It was like a living thing as it drifted across the landscape.

Arms slowly flailing
They march across the skyline
Wind turbine giants

This put me in mind of Cervante's aged hero Don Quixote "tilting at windmills" believing that they are giants.

This ramshackle ruin
It's untended garden now
Is home to fox cubs

Uneven slabs cross
A lazy flowing river
Life ebbs slowly by

Early Morning

I have always been an early riser, which has afforded me plenty of opportunity to appreciate the quiet and stillness before the rest of the world wakes. There is definitely something ghostlike, a theme which runs through many of these haiku.

Daylight creeps over
A sleeping world Is revealed
Ghostly world recedes

Stillness hangs over
A ghostly world in slumber
Birds begin to chirp

Sun stirs gentle mist

Across a lake serenely
A new day begins

A particularly striking sunrise over a local lake gave rise to this verse. The rising sun, warming the waters, gave rise to vapour lifting off the lake.

Morning stillness hangs
Upon a world bathed in sun
Hope again renewed

Each day is an opportunity to start afresh.

Birds twitter and tweet
In darkness even the sun
Is still fast asleep

A golden dawn breaks
Endless possibilities
The sleeper awakes

"The sleeper awakes" is a phrase from Frank Herbert's sci fi epic **Dune**, and relates to the awakening of the hero Paul's prescient powers. Perhaps the phrase was in mind due to the imminent release of Denis Villeneuve's much anticipated movie remake.

Dew drops sparkling
The world stirring to life
A new day begins

Sunlight enraptured
In diamond sparkling dew
A new day begins

A carpet of dew
Sparkling diamond droplets
Reflect rising sun

The sunlight shining brightly through early morning dew on the grass looks especially like a scattering of diamonds.

A heavy grey still
Rests oppressively upon
A world at slumber

Morning rain stirs me
From dull and anxious dreaming
A grey day begins

I was attempting to capture that sense that maybe you have been laying half awake for hours listening to the rain, not wanting to get up to face a dreary day.

As daylight seeps in
Cold rain drums upon the roof
Lamenting summer

Pale orange street lights
Punctuate cold morning mist
Fox crossing the road

A golden sunrise
To the sound of dawn's chorus
And soft pigeon calls

Early morning hush
World bathed in sodium light
The clock ticks loudly

A new day dawning
Reflecting on past mistakes
Hope for the future

Zen Garden Disappointment

Visiting a much hyped "Zen garden" tourist attraction we discovered that the "tea room" was in fact the owner's conservatory, adjacent to their private kitchen, from which was drifting the aroma I can only describe as being like dog food being reheated in a microwave.

I hope to find peace
But find it just too tacky
In this Happy Land

I hope to find Zen
But it smells of hot dog food
In this Happy Land

I was disappointed to observe that although some parts of the garden were delightful, other areas were a little tacky and overdone or just bizarre. I couldn't shake the smell of hot dog food.

Pure Land Buddhism is a broad branch of Mahayana Buddhism. Happy Land is used here to suggest the idea of a theme park.

The image is actually from the beautiful and tranquil Japanese Garden at Newquay, Cornwall, and not the Zen garden concerned.

Night Terrors

Tendrils of thick smoke
Man intruding my bedroom
Nocturnal terrors

I am sometimes awoken by half imagined figures standing over me as I lay in bed, dark and sinister shadows hovering against the roof, or the belief that the house is on fire.

Night terrors more commonly occur in children and typically happen at that border between sleep and waking, where we are becoming aware of the real world, but our imaginations are still powerfully constructing images. They can be the result of sleep deprivation, medication or anxiety. A number of studies, from USA, China and Greece have concluded that approximately 40% of the population have experienced some form of sleep disturbance or sleep disorder as a result of COVID-19 related anxiety and worry.

Ancient Monuments

In far ancient times
Did they hold such mystery
Stonehenge monoliths

Prehistoric tourists
Did they bring their own
Pre-packed lunches

The visitor centre was only built in recent decades so naturally ancient day trippers would have had to bring their own food.

Two sphinxes staring
A century they played this game
Both have yet to blink

A gift from the stars
Mysterious monolith
Aliens use rivets?

In 2020 a number of mysterious metal monoliths, reminiscent of those from the film 2001, appeared in remote locations around the world. Their exact source was unknown, and most disappeared just as mysteriously soon after. Whatever their origin, one thing was clear: they had obviously been constructed using very terrestrial technologies. Like rivets.

Halloween

We have often had a lot of fun and really pushed the boat out and put on a fantastic show for the local children on Halloween. However during Covid we did not want to encourage the delightful little snot gobblers to be roaming door to door, smearing their unwashed hands over everything and spreading the virus.

Halloween season
Keep your disease to yourselves
Foul little monsters

The Skies

In the azure skies
Lines fading, dissipating
Memory of a jet

Though I walk for miles
He never seems much nearer
The pale daylight moon

Whispy stream of cloud
Flowing through an azure sky
No sound but birdsong

Against bitter skies
Metal cars wheeling through space
Accompanied by gulls

We visited the rather run down seafront at Great Yarmouth where a huge wheel dominates the skyline. It is one of those sprawling British seaside towns that sadly looks like it's glory days are long passed. It is now an uncomfortable combination of boarded up buildings, lap dancing clubs and tacky amusement arcades.

Seen From My Hot Tub

As is often the case, I tried the same idea with some minor changes.

Bathed in hot water
Watching leaves sway overhead
Clear Summer evening

Bathed in hot water
Watching birds wheel overhead
Clear Summer evening

Seen from my hot tub
A Japanese lantern sits
By a still koi pond

Beneath swirling waters
Strobing disco lights, close encounters
Of the hot tub kind

A placid koi pond
Reflects a silvery sky
Birds reel overhead

On Royalty

> Does our Monarch think
> The whole world smells like fresh paint?
> Asking for a friend

It is only natural that wherever the Queen is scheduled to travel, the locals will want to present themselves and their town in the best possible light. It does raise the question though, whether everywhere the Queen goes there is the aroma of fresh paint. Perhaps she thinks this is how the entire country smells.

This following mischievous verse is about cultural misunderstandings on several levels.

> Sultan to the Prince:
> "Monkeys in a gilded cage
> Don't eat all at once"

After hearing that Sir David Attenborough and Prince William had been working together on conservation projects I imagined a fictional dialogue between our future monarch and one from an entirely different culture. It is intended to shock and provoke by challenging cultural and racial stereotypes and expectations, whilst at the same time drawing on them for humour.

It has long been tradition for gifts and tokens of goodwill to be made between dignitaries, monarchs and heads of state, and for much of it's life the Tower of London became the depository for unwanted wild animals. From 1200s to 1835 it housed a menagerie of exotic wild animals including lions and a polar bear. In this imagined scenario a gift of monkeys has been made in a beautiful, ornate cage. One might think that this is a splendid, if unusual and impractical, gift of exotic pets until it is understood they were actually supplied as a delicacy for eating.

On a Theme of Ageing

Scrawny ancient cat
Blackened lips, unsteady legs
Summer days must end

My neighbour's mature cat became unusually sociable and friendly over the Spring and Summer months. But like the Summer itself, all life has it's seasons and nothing is forever. Sadly this friendly little being didn't see out the Winter. The following verses continue this seasonal metaphor for human life.

Our time is so short
Seasons in the shifting rain
Kindness costs nothing

Our time is so short

Blown about by season's winds
Kindness costs nothing

Be grateful daily
Dancing in the summer rain
Waters the spirit

I find something quite romantic and uninhibited about the idea of dancing in the rain.

How the years fly by
He doesn't recognise me -
Man in the mirror

Lamenting lost youth
The old man in the mirror
Reflects life like mine

Youthful pale skin marked
Ruptured, creased by passing years
Ageing leaves it's mark

This could equally apply to an ageing person rather than the graceful silver birch tree that inspired it.

We all wear our history writ large on and in our skin. Unless you pay for expensive plastic surgery, in which case you may be a 90 year old with eyes on either side of your head and a bulldog clip at the back of your neck defiantly holding back gravity and nature.

My mind remembers
Days of boundless energy
That my legs forgot

As we age we will all find that our bodies become less enthusiastic than our minds, and that rather than being refreshed after a night's sleep we feel like we've been kicked about by a horse.

A night mare?

After the long night

I awake to the new day
Full of aches and pain

Concerning Donald Trump

I am not a fan of Donald Trump or his brand of populist politics or ridiculous self-aggrandizement. I apologise if this differs from your own political viewpoint, but he is not particularly admired beyond the borders of the USA, as evidenced by the Baby Trump blimp, and the damage that has been done to long standing international relationships. Trumpists should probably skip this section.

> Shower him in gold
> This narcissist President
> Stormy times ahead

Here I am referencing a number of the scandals surrounding the 45th US President, particularly the Stormy Daniels affair and the "Russia pee tape" allegations from the Steele Dossier. There are also allusions to the man's greed and apparent malignant narcissism.

> Is that a bad wig
> On orange man-baby's head?

Concealing no brain!

Perhaps there is a reason for the bizarre hair. What is it hiding?

An orange baboon
In a tacky gold White House
So much Covfefe

This includes an obvious reference to Trump's now infamous nonsense Covfefe tweet. Did he fall asleep typing that on the toilet?

An orange baboon
In a tacky gold White House
It seems hate Trumps love

It is said that once you raise the spectre of the Nazis or Adolf Hitler, then you have de-facto lost the argument. However, as philosopher and Harvard professor George Santayana is oft quoted, "Those who cannot remember the past are condemned to repeat it."

In Twenty Twenty
The radicalised Reich wing
Trumps America

You cant spell "hatred"
It's a universal fact
Without "red" and "hat"

They have hate for those
Who do not speak their language
Or better than them

In 666 syllables:

Presidential debate
Like watching mud flinging in
An old folks care home

So the poop was flung
No knockout blow was landed
Trump's mic not switched off

In the age of Trump
Americans overseas
Fake Canadians

Dull ape in a mask
May look somewhat ludicrous
Less likely to spread

Ignore health warnings
At super spreader events
Trump's America

In September 2020 Trump held an event in the Rose Garden at the White House to announce the nomination of his Supreme Court Justice pick, Amy Coney Barrett. The event was packed, with people huddled closely together, not wearing masks and not practicing any social distancing measures. Naturally it became a COVID super spreader event with a significant number of attendees later testing positive for the virus.

"Maybe I'm immune
Must be due to my great genes"
"Will you just shut up"

After being hospitalized with the virus Trump boasted that his quick recovery must be due to his great genes rather than the cocktails of experimental drugs made available to him. During one of the Presidential debates Jo Biden had snapped at Trump's constant interruptions and attempts to talk over him.

In 666 syllables:

Runs rings around me how
This mask-less orange ape
I've never seen Trump run

Someone on social media told me that "Trump could run rings around you." The obvious retort almost wrote itself. The man doesn't do exercise. Of any kind.

Not voting Trump today
His failings run so deep
No U.S. citizen

Naturally, not being a US citizen, I was not entitled to vote in the Presidential election.

Decency won out
We can take a breath again
Love in fact Trumps hate

And just like that, I was again able to enjoy a peaceful night's sleep without worrying that someone would recklessly start a nuclear war with an ill-informed, badly spelled Tweet. The adults were back in the room.

And yet the insanity was not over with the election...

Washington on fire
Flames of outrage fanned by
A vile orange ape

Capitol idea
Idiotic President
Pours petrol on the flames

Cthulhu and the Works of HP Lovecraft

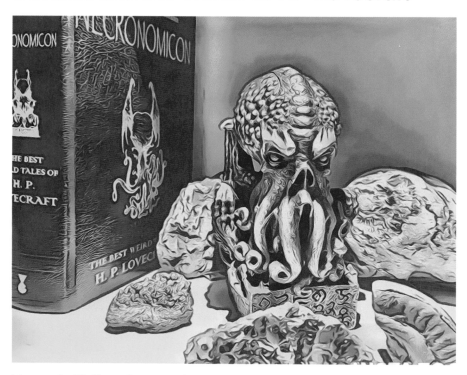

Howard Philips Lovecraft is one of the most influential and significant writers of horror fiction in the early 20th Century and is cited as the inspiration for such notable authors as Ramsay Campbell, Brian Lumley, Stephen King and many others. Amongst his most well known creations is the fictional Necronomicon and the short story **The Call of Cthulhu** in which a huge, squid-headed, hulking elder god sleeps in his ancient sunken city R'lyeh. Predating humanity, he awaits the day when the stars are correctly aligned so that he can again rise from beneath the waves and reclaim the Earth as his own, driving humanity insane. His dreams leak into the minds of feeble men, pushing them to madness and suicide.

I read a collection of Lovecraft and Cthulhu related haiku, **Haiku and Other Mythos Madness**, compiled by Lester Smith and was inspired to try my own tributes.

Towering mountain

Dreams of reawakening
Beneath the black waves

Mountain that walked
Sleeping in his charnel house
Dreams insanity

It spirals beyond
The murder, madness, mayhem
As Great Cthulhu dreams

Horror realised:
Let monstrous sleeping gods lie
Beneath ceaseless waves

This is a play on the phrase "let sleeping dogs lie".

On Children

Kite tails fluttering
Soaring like a dancing bird
A child's joyous face

Kite tails fluttering
Flapping like a dancing bird
Children on a hill

As I conceived these, I saw them as being witnessed from the point of view of the kite, looking down on the children from above. The children are totally lost in the pleasure of flying their kites.

Cries of whiney brats
Haunt English Heritage sites
Adult only days?

Sat beneath a tree
Is the soundtrack to my hell
Other people's kids?

I have often wondered if these tourist sites should perhaps offer "adults only" days.

Whilst it is considered polite to coo and make adoring noises when meeting someone with a new born child, unfortunately some look like something out of a 1970s horror film, that only a mother could truly love!

Other people's kids
Sometimes ugly little things
Best to hold your tongue

Someone has to love
These ugly little monsters
Other people's kids

The healing power
Of a child's gleeful laughter
Given most freely

And yet there is magic in hearing the sound of infant children gurgling with laughter.

Remembrance

Yellow flowers grow
Where once soldiers fought and died
Time subdued them all

Written on the site of a 13th century castle and battle field where many men fell and died. No-one now remembers who they were, or what they fought for.

Only ruins now
Where brothers once slept and worked

Dark rooks cross the sky

The verse above was inspired while roaming around the ruins of the at Fountains Abbey in North Yorkshire, one of the largest and best preserved ruined Cistercian monasteries in England.

These bravest young men
Return to their mothers' arms
In wooden caskets

A grey winter day
We still commemorate them
And their sacrifice

No one now alive
Can remember who they were
Toppled grave markers

Wandering through an overgrown graveyard I was struck that nobody living cared about those who were buried there, or had any recollection of who they had been.

The Night Skies

I can recall when I was younger that I could look up into the night sky and clearly see where the Milky Way cut a dusty swathe through the sky. Due to light pollution it is increasingly something which younger generations have missed out on. Being able to see millions of stars with the naked eye helps us to appreciate our place in the cosmos, and understanding that each is a sun which might have it's own potentially life supporting planets gives us a sense of the immensity of the universe.

Starry winter skies
Underneath Orion's Belt
Orion's trousers

Silvery moon light
Undulates in gentle waves
Pale cherry blossom

Under moonlit skies
It is snowing soft pink flakes
Cherry blossom ghosts

Shimmering starlight
Perhaps someone is out there
Looking back at me

Dark shadows huddled
Across a silent landscape
New moon's sideways smile

I quite like the idea that the crescent moon is in fact a smile in the sky.

In afternoon glare
Past the hazy fields of wheat
The silvery moon

The Meaning and Transience of Life

Forever onward
Always shorter than one thinks
Life's transient journey

Simple honest truth:
Life is mostly nutrition
Some inhalation

A day in the sun
Such frail and transient beauty

Is gone tomorrow

Every image lost
Distilled moments of beauty
Like tears in rain

This last line recalls the Rutger Hauer "Tears in rain" monologue at the end of the film Blade Runner. Here his character Roy Batty, an android who has become tragically and fearfully aware of his own mortality, is in mourning for what will be lost forever in the moment of his death. It is a truth that after we have gone, we take all those unique instants that only we witnessed, with us.

The meaning of life
To be happy and healthy
Perhaps forty two

And in another science fiction influenced haiku I recall the meaning of life from **The Hitchhiker's Guide To the Galaxy** by Douglas Adams.

Seasons cycle on
Like hand removed from water
The ghost that was you

Each single vision
Private, personal, unique
Be grateful each day

Each precious moment
Only you experienced
You take it with you

These following are all about how insignificant we are in the greater scheme of things. And yet because we are such fleeting, short lived things, that is what makes us also so special and precious.

Each single being
Every single living soul
All dust in the wind

Each single being
That ever walked the earth
All dust in the wind

Often things unplanned:
Moments arise unbidden
Out of the ether

Remember me for
The size of my immense heart
And not my ego

The things you most love
No matter how hard you try
They all go away

The things you most love
No cast iron guarantees
They return your love

With this last verse, I actually had in mind someone eating a box of chocolates. No matter how much they love chocolate, the chocolate will never, ever return that love. Sometimes the things we love only do us harm.

All things are transient
Nothing can last forever
Except perhaps death

Move along the bus
Make some more room for others
A baby is born

This is all about the idea of the "circle of life", that for every one who dies, another life takes their place.

I stare sadly at
A chocolate bar wrapper
Funny how things go

Childhood accident

Is my life now just images
In a flash forward?

As a child I was knocked down by a car. With the Hollywood
obsession with flash forwards I wondered if perhaps the life I have
lived is just a flash forward from that moment.

A constellation
Each one dazzling and brilliant
We are made of stars

You come from nothing
Live a brief but frantic life
Then back to star dust

My life haunted by
Dreams of things I never did
A lot like sleeping

This one is intentionally vague and ambiguous. You bring to it your
own interpretation.

Microbial life
On the face of a pebble
Human existence

Life boils and bubbles
Thrives in primordial soup
Want bread rolls with that?

I imagined a truck driver in a roadside greasy spoon café being
deep and philosophical, only to interrupted in his contemplations by
the waitress.

Love and Romance

Intense love for you
Expressed as plastic roses
From a petrol station

Clearly someone has forgotten to buy a thoughtful Valentines Day gift and had to settle for the best on offer at the all night petrol station. Nothing says "I love you" quite like a piece of plastic crap.

A playwrite once said
Better to have loved and lost
All the world's a stage

The image above is a statue of the English playwrite William Shakespeare, which stands outside his birthplace in Stratford-Upon-

Avon. So many phrases in common usage in the English language derived from Shakespeare plays.

Big Bird

This gigantic bird
Always remains the same size
Despite the ice cold

With apologies for another wicked and puerile attempt at humour. Yes, it is about what you think it is about.

The image is of the "Pop Galo" installation from Portuguese artist Joana Vasconcelos displayed at the Yorkshire Sculpture Park.

Wentworth Castle Visit

Wentworth Castle is another property managed by the National Trust, near Barnsley, in Yorkshire. It was home to Royal diplomat Thomas Wentworth who was outraged when his cousin inherited his family home, Wentworth Woodhouse in 1695.

Another family whose wealth was derived in part from links to the slave trade, the house is impressive and the gardens and surrounding parklands, full of deer, are substantial. They include a huge mock castle folly.

Ancient castle walls
Glimpsed through the dappled trees
One man's folly

Massive ancient tree
Gnarled limbs reaching for the sun
Marking years like hours

A flower garden
Beds of radiant colour
Pensioners planted

The pensioners didn't plant the beds of flowers. The pensioners are planted on the benches around the garden. Good luck trying to move them.

This rich man's folly
Temple to excess and wealth
Built on slavery

Wentworth was one of the principal negotiators of the Treaty of Utrecht, which secured Britain as the supplier of slaves to the Spanish colonies.

Inspired By Film and Television

An old bird warbling
Through the dark and misery
C'est La Vie en Rose

The film La Vie en Rose is a highly acclaimed, award-winning biopic of the iconic French singer Edith Piaf. Unfortunately it is also the unrelentingly bleak and miserable story of someone who appeared to be unforgivably rude and obnoxious to everyone. There is a duality in this haiku, as with so many, it could equally be about a song bird taking part in the early dawn chorus.

Sequins and prancing
Not Strictly for everyone
Stick it up your arse

If I had a catch phrase it would be "stick it up your arse." Irreverent, disrespectful and witty.

I am of an age where I vaguely remember the television show Come Dancing, from the Blackpool Tower Ballroom with Angela Ripon. It was full of geriatrics twirling round the dance floor to tinny organ music, and rightfully condemned to late evenings on BBC2. So it is a constant bemusement and mystery to me that the show has been successfully revived as Strictly Come Dancing (or Dancing With The Stars) and enjoys phenomenal success. The combination of high camp outfits, and po-faced judges making meaningless statements like "your line needs to be more fluid", is just not my cup of tea. And to make matters worse, every BBC television and radio presenter seems to think that everybody else MUST share their rabid enthusiasm. I would rather gouge my eyes out with rusty spoons. And when was the last time you saw ANYBODY doing a Tango, Foxtrot or Paso Doble down the local nightspot? They would get lynched.

Praying it will stop
Watching Strictly Come Dancing
Poncing in sequins

Dimpled down under
Four thousand pounds of beauty!
What a silly arse

This verse came after watching a UK Channel 4 television documentary where a woman was paying £4000 pounds for cosmetic surgery to reshape her posterior. It seemed a particularly ridiculous and extravagant way to spend money.

Is "wabi sabi"
The reason why I so loved
The second Death Star?

"Wabi sabi" is a Japanese concept. "Wabi" is a quality of something which is imperfect but appreciated for it's flaws. "Sabi" relates to an ageing quality, such as a patina or a sheen which develops over time. So "Wabi sabi" is a beauty or value something has or acquires through it's age and imperfections. This seems to me to perfectly describe the unfinished second Death Star in The Return of the Jedi.

Fog

From out of the fog
To the surprise of us both
A startled pheasant

Road goes ever on
Of this I am quite certain
Though I can't see it

In thick morning mist
Coughing shadows pass me by
My breath a small cloud

Looming from the mist
Coughing shadows pass me by
Corona virus threat

On a Theme of Insomnia

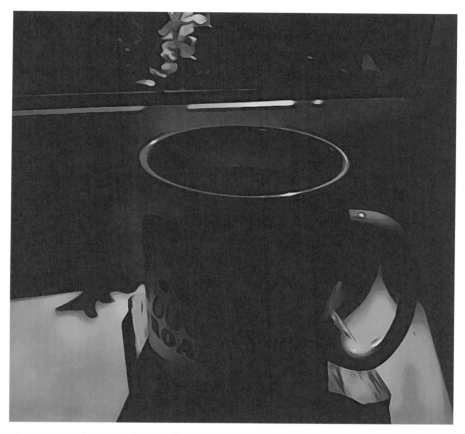

From time to time I find it difficult to switch off and go to sleep, no matter how physically tired, and so spend the early morning hours listening to the relentless, oppressive ticking of the clock. I have tried to catch the essence of insomnia in the following verses.

Not even pale moon
Lights this still, midnight blackness
Sleep so evasive

A thunderous clock
Steals these precious hours of sleep
Still Blackness outside

Drinking cherry tea
As around me others sleep
Midnight blackness rules

The kitchen clock ticks
Measures out every second
As others slumber

Sleep impossible
With your head an airless box
These first world problems

Three in the morning
Each restless waking second
Is ten minutes long

In the dark small hours
I lay awake and listen
To the sound of rain

Life's Unanswered Questions

Haiku developed out of the Japanese tradition of Renga, word game parties and competitions where participants would try to demonstrate their wit and wisdom through short verses, trying to out-do each other, often linked to those of the previous participant. It certainly does not have to be serious. **The Penguin Book of Haiku,** compiled by Adam Kern particularly appears to have been curated to be provocative and is full of verses covering crudity, bodily functions and sex.

Here's a bit of mischievous toilet humour of my own:

> Poo on the knuckles
> How's that even possible
> Asking for a friend

The Horrors of Customer Service

> Online banking help
> Enough to make you see red
> Give you no credit
>
> Online banking help
> Enough to make your blood boil
> Not much help at all

On a holiday cruise around the Mediterranean, I awoke in the middle of the night to discover that we had made an unscheduled stop at an industrial port in Spain. As we manoeuvred into dock, we were met by a convoy of flashing blue lights. Shortly after, it appeared that a passenger and his luggage were discretely offloaded into an awaiting ambulance. I speculated what a clumsy, insensitive customer service might write by way of an apology. I imagine that many passengers awoke the next morning blissfully unaware of the night's events.

> We're sorry to hear
> Your holiday was cut short
> By your death at sea
>
> Arseholes and elbows
> Do the power companies
> Know the difference?

On Bonsai

Miniature trees
Contorted by hand and wire
"Natural" beauty

I like the irony of this verse, that by extreme artifice we are trying to create something that is natural looking. The art of bonsai is all about creating a stylized image of an ideal tree in miniature. This is done with horticultural techniques such as wiring and pruning, and is not, as many people believe, a particular dwarf species of tree.

The alliteration, or repeated "t" sound in this following haiku made me laugh as I was composing it.

> The art of bonsai
> Turning a twig
> Into a twee*

* twee

/twiː/

adjective BRITISH
excessively or affectedly quaint, pretty, or sentimental.

> Horse chestnut bonsai
> Conquer growing habit, leaves
> Like dinner plates

> Rows of tiny trees
> A forest in my garden
> In ceramic pots

> Truly makes no sense
> Abducting trees from the wild
> Would be vandalism

In the bonsai hobby, many of the older, more prized trees were "collected from the wild", known as "yamadori". This is not a practice I am particularly comfortable or happy with. Unless the collector has the express permission of the land owner, and the trees are destined to be destroyed, perhaps because of planned development work, it seems rather arrogant to think that we can just help ourselves for selfish reasons to something that has germinated, rooted and grown in that spot.

> Uneven blue glaze
> My favourite bonsai pot
> So wabi sabi

> Lost in the forest

Amid bare trunks I wander
My Zen place of calm

Forest canopy
Trees stand white beneath fresh snow
Bonsai in winter

Wintery paradise
This garden created with love
Snow, bonsai and koi

In decades from now
This featureless Hornbeam stump
Will be fine bonsai

In bonsai it is not uncommon to take a taller tree and cut it down significantly and regrow the branches over subsequent years. Here, I have taken a six foot tall hornbeam tree which I bought cheaply from a garden centre and cut it down to a five inch, featureless stump. Done at the right time of year, it will throw out new branches in spring, and the years of training, development and refinement to become a spectacular, miniature bonsai tree begin.

Amid frozen trees
I sit, breathe and contemplate
The nature of truth

Here I am sat, not in some wooded glade, but in my garden amongst my collection of bonsai trees.

On the Theme of Sheep

Beneath Easter skies
A whispy cloud of sheep drifts
Across a green field

I liked this imagery of a flock of sheep as a fluffy white cloud, drifting rather than walking across the field, just as a cloud would.

Mournful calls of "Dave"
"Dave". A heart-breaking chorus
From a field of sheep

Once heard, it can never be unheard, but their calls sound chillingly human.

On my commute:
Black sheep doing yoga
On a grassy knoll

On a drive in to work through the beautiful rural village of Flockton, I found myself pulled up at traffic lights. Immediately to my left was a little grassy hill with a group of sheep, each with their forelegs bent, grazing, like people doing the "downward dog" yoga pose.

A field with no sheep
Like farmers without wellies
Each to his own (kind)

This is my somewhat cheeky reference to bestiality and farming stereotypes. Move along now...

Smart Devices and Technology

It knows your full name
And your innermost desires
Careless talk costs lives

"Careless talk costs lives" was a propaganda term used during the war. In this era of smart devices, it can accidentally order cat food or switch on or off smart devices. It is always listening... it knows all your secrets, including those you might not want your nearest and dearest to know.

It knows your full name
And your most secret desires
Your id up for sale

Like the ship's computer HAL in the film 2001, is there something a little sinister about a technological device in our homes that is listening to everything that we do?

On Cats

A sleeping cat
Paws twitching for
Invisible mice

Animal and human watcher Desmond Morris in his book **Catwatching** asserts that we keep cats in a somewhat artificial state of dual personality. Because we mother them and provide for their care, we feed and shelter them, they will show kitten-like behaviours in our presence. They will mew in a tone which sounds like a baby's cry(which is a trait they perform especially for humans), and they will knead us when being held as though still suckling. In that moment they have regressed back to kittenhood and a state of dependency. But they are also independent, natural predators with instincts to chase and kill, despite the fact that they no longer need to do so for food. It can sometimes be shocking for cat owners to see their docile, loving pet become a ferocious killer in an instant.

> Green Foliage stirs
> Cat approaches stealthily
> Hisses and cat slaps

This verse came after watching one of my cats stalking across the garden, and my other cat pouncing out of the undergrowth. A session of cat slapping followed before one retreated.

> Apex predator
> Vicious killer honed for death
> Sleeps the day away

> Sing your proud heart out
> Robin, bobbing on the fence
> A rare treat for cats

We used to have a friendly little robin that would visit and sit on the fence chirping his fierce little heart out. One day, one of my neighbours called to me in the garden over the fence, and said that she was a little concerned that the cats might get at a nest in the nearby hedging. As she was telling me this, I was surreptitiously brushing aside a broken shell with my foot to hide the incriminating evidence. We never did see that robin again.

> Lazy Sunday noon
> Rain drums conservatory roof
> Cat washes her face

> Little furry gifts
> Don't think that I'm ungrateful
> Presents from my cat

I have a theory that cats and dogs become surrogate children for those without kids. We lavish on them the care and attention we might otherwise give a child, and they become a cherished member of the family. We even call them our "fur babies". Some even celebrate their birthdays or buy them Christmas gifts. You tread on very thin ice if you suggest "it's just a cat" when visiting someone.

That cat lives there, and you are just a guest.

Healing frequency
A softly purring engine
Cuddles with my cat

Gently humming with
The frequency of healing
Cuddles and cat hugs

Relaxing mindful breaths
A soothing meditation
Blissful purring cat

A chance encounter
Not all new friends have two legs
Parting is sorrow

We visited the stately home of Sizergh Castle in Helsington, Cumbria and found a friendly black cat sleeping on a bench in the walled kitchen garden. As luck would have it, we found ourselves there again exactly a year to the day. And the friendly cat was there waiting.

Glittering green eyes
Warm, soft, downy fur humming
Cuddles with my cat

Curtains subtle twitch
Eyes watching my every move
Nosey cat observes

Does she dream of me
The faithful love of my life?
My beautiful cat

Nothing gets a cat owner out of bed faster than the sound of a retching cat.

On the carpet now
Matted balls of fur and bile

Presents from my cat

So the saying goes
A cat may look at a king
Same goes for sunrise

They hunt together
These sleek creatures honed to kill
For Dreamies cat treats

Drumming on the stairs
The thunder of tiny feet
Cats playing at tig

A Mysterious Woodland Gathering

In a wooded glade
Dancing with weird abandon
White hooded figures

I am fortunate to live on the edge of the suburbs with rolling countryside, country parks and woodland on the doorstep. Working from home, one lunchtime I felt the need to get out and stretch my legs and suggested a walk to my partner of a couple of miles and off we set - up and down quiet local country lanes.

As we walked along a quiet road, admiring the autumnal colours in the trees, we heard what I initially took to be children's voices in the wood off to my left. In a clearing, where there is a disused quarry set back from the road I could see white robed figures dancing and chanting. They were adults, some distance through the trees, and somewhat indistinct. I climbed an earth banking at the side of the road try to get a better look and at this point I took a picture. What were clearly adults, dressed in white robes, were moving in a circle clockwise, and singing what sounded like an ululating African tribal song - think of the residents on Kong's Skull Island chanting. Their swaying dance put me in mind of President Trump's recent Saudi Arabian swaying sword dance as they circled round. There were somewhere in the region of ten participants.

As I continued down the lane they passed from view, but we could still vaguely hear them for a few moments. I was tempted to investigate further but also worried about offending or interrupting some social gathering, and equally unsettled by what looked like some pagan ritual in a remote spot. It certainly crossed my mind that this is how horror films start - with people blundering into mysterious rituals in isolated spots.

The gathering was on a Friday lunchtime and one of my initial thoughts was to ask who gathers in the distant woods for some ritual at lunchtime on a working day? My next thoughts were naturally that there seemed to be no regard for Covid precautions in force at the time, rules on large gatherings or appropriate social distancing. Being some way from civilisation my thoughts naturally ran to The Wicker Man and the recent Midsommar film. There certainly seemed to be something pagan about the event.

The spot was in a disused quarry in woodland. To this day the event remains something of a mystery to me. I regret that my courage failed me and I didn't venture to investigate this strange occurrence further at the time. I have revisited the site a couple of times since but found no clues to what was going on or who those white robed mystery figures were..

The picture at the top of this section is my shot through the tangled woods of the group.

Deserted quarry
Quiet now where witches danced
With wild abandon

In a wooded dell
Twisted tree limbs reaching out
Could it be magic

Snow and silence now
Where once the witches danced

Too cold for Sabbath

Moss

Moss is a beautiful and much under appreciated plant. It has a multitude of varieties from plush, velvet looking clump mosses to horizontal growing varieties. They come in a rich variety of shades of green, and can be found on old walls, trees, rotting stumps and damp, shaded surfaces.

Velvet moss glistens
Red fronds salute the sun
Soft sound of birdsong

I greatly admire
Your green verdant velvet sleeve
Moss enveloped branch

On the Theme of Flat Earth

It amuses me endlessly that the Flat Earth Society website claims to have members all round the globe. Their lack of understanding of basic physics, and my love and appreciation of sunsets inspired several haiku.

Red fiery orb sinks
Beyond undulating waves
But not on flat Earth

On this spheroid Earth
Some people think it is flat
Some brains must be too

Falling into light
Golden rays envelop me
As the world rotates

The image above is a sunset photographed from the lighthouse at

Cape St Vincent (cabo são vicente) in Portugal, the most Easterly point of Europe. Watching the sun setting and disappearing below the visible horizon is not possible on a flat Earth.

The Evils of Social Media

Increasingly we are slaves to our online life – posting social media updates and videos: on Facebook, Instagram, TikTok and whatever the current, in vogue platform is. We obsess about he we look, what we are eating, where we are visiting, who is following us, or how many likes we received. We all have our cliques and favourite silos of information or safe spaces that we retreat to, and where our beliefs and viewpoints are re-inforced by like minded people. We feel uncomfortable when we are challenged or personally attacked. We have a tendency to argue back in a forum which is designed to promote clicks, views and adversarial content, and where provocative material is rewarded. I fear that it is leading to an insular, ironically disconnected society with a lack of civility. It is scary to think that there are generations now who have never lived without the ills or addictions of social media.

In his book **Ten Arguments For Deleting Your Social Media Accounts Right Now**, Jaron Lanier advocates that we should abandon social media for our own benefit and that of society as a whole. Even when we are in the company of others, we are often more involved with our phones, and obsessively checking for updates like crack addicts. At the very least, we need to learn how to switch off our phones and engage fully with the real world, rather than the online illusion, and be more present in the here and now. It will make us better human beings if we do.

The image above is a statue of a Greek goddess which stands in the gardens of Brodsworth Hall, near Doncaster in the United Kingdom. The white figure looks particularly striking against the flame red leaves of the Japanese maple tree in it's autumnal finery. The figure hiding behind a mask seemed an appropriate metaphor for our online personas, a curated digital mask we wear to present ourselves to the digital world.

The following are my cynical observations and thoughts concerning social media, our addiction to it, and the emotional damage it can do.

Welcome to the internet
Brings out the best in people
And the very worst

This book of faces
Makes none a better version
Unlike a real book

This book of faces
Makes none a better person
It's not a real book

Her sensitive soul
Bared on social media
Perils of Facebook

Friends who never met
Do they really exist?

Only on Facebook

It seems that there is a desperate need to accumulate clicks or likes on social media, or to have the greater number of followers or friends. It is a measure of our popularity. But social media has a global reach and often those friends of followers are people we may have never met in real life – they wouldn't even recognize us if they passed us in the street. A wise person once told me that a true friend is someone that you can call at 2am and they will be there for you in your hour of need. I'm not sure that this can be said of our many Facebook friends.

Furious tweeting
Hidden up amongst the trees
There's no Twitter here

Our digital life is managed and curated by us – the images we use, the posts and updates we broadcast. I am particularly guilty of sometimes making posts which are intentionally provocative, and which do not necessarily represent my truly held beliefs. This verse is about whether people take the bait and believe what they read and respond to these posts.

If I set a trap
Will you blunder into it?
Now over to you...

Quite often I find myself regretting what I have posted on social media, and, kicking myself for stirring up a hornets' nest, have to delete my post or leave a particular online group or forum for fear of the angry mob. Perhaps I have become victim to my own trap.

On Writing Haiku

Haiku writing initially developed from playful and witty word games played amongst the Japanese literati. It is this spirit that draws me to it, as well as the Zen mindful sense of capturing a beautiful and vivid snapshot of a moment it time. I draw my inspiration from a host of sources and influences including familiar sayings, song lyrics, film quotes and poetic phrases which become lodged in my mind. It is then a matter of wrangling those into a verse of three lines and 17 syllables. Occasionally I will vary in the syllable count, but usually do so consciously, and with valid reason. Often I will try different combinations or phrases until I am happy with the result.

The haiku here are not only about the joy of writing haiku, but also about the dangers of ego and vanity which can come from receiving praise.

Haiku distractions
Witticisms and wise word play
Real work is postponed

Tiny insect crawls
Across a page of verse
Enjoying haiku?

I am most humbled
Your praise appreciated
Oh, Queen of Haiku

Oh, Queen of Haiku
You created a monster
In three lines of verse

Such wit and wisdom
In seventeen syllables
I love a Haiku

A picture painted
In seventeen syllables
I love a Haiku

A vignette painted
In seventeen syllables
God loves a trier

A Haiku posted
Glowing plaudits are received
Ego monster born

Through this thoughtful praise
A monster was created
Damn pride and ego

Keep writing they said
Persevere as well they said
Look who's laughing now!

Or perhaps crying now that you have fed the ego monster. Who knows where it will all end.

> My grocery list
> However so lyrical
> Is not a haiku

I must have got out of the wrong side of bed on this day. This was my retort at seeing numerous postings on online groups of poems and verses of all kinds. Whatever they were, however skillfully they were crafted, and evocative in their imagery, they were not haiku.

Birds

Struts like a proud king
Radiant regal magpie
Feathers green and blue

Trilling in a tree
Singing his tiny heart out
Red breasted robin

Have you ever heard ducks suddenly all quacking together. It sounds like a chorus of laughter. Makes you wonder what they find so funny. Do they know something we don't?

Breaking the silence
Raucous laughter of ducks
Must be my bad jokes?

Breaking the silence
Loud raucous laughter of ducks
Gulls hysterical

In a briar patch
He sits still and watches me
Red breasted robin

The cats brought in a thrush which I had to rescue. I could feel it's tiny heart thumping in it's chest as it was nestled in my hands.

Tiny beating heart
Nestled safely in my hand
Fly free little bird

Regret and Alcohol

Early morning dark
Young ladies totter home drunk
In crumpled dresses

After the night out
Staggering home in disgrace
Drunk and regretful

In early darkness
Young men propped against walls
In drunken slumber

The image is of The Good Samaritan statue that stands outside Dewsbury Town Hall, in the northern market town. It has been pointed out that it looks like a pair of drunks helping each other home after a particularly heavy night.

On Work

Occupied by ghosts
Empty chairs at empty desks
Office in lockdown

With the total absence of staff the office feels eerie and unsettling.

Silence and greyness
The office: end of lockdown
Desks still and empty

Secret Santa fun
My colleagues don't much know me

They are all Muslim

This is my tongue firmly in cheek observation of celebrating Christmas in an office where I am now the only one who does. Although considered "haram", my colleagues indulge me, for which I am eternally grateful. In my defence, I consider it a seasonal team bonding exercise, rather than any kind of religious observance.

Let down by colleagues
My fears made reality
Manager's burden

Unfortunately there is only one of us, whoever we are, and so we must delegate work to others and trust that they will exercise the same high level of skill, professionalism and perfection that we would. Sometimes we are asking too much and that trust is misplaced...

A soothing hot bath
To ease off the working day
On my own clock now

Busy workers pass
Amid the drying grasses
Ant society

Their daily commute
Busy rushing to and fro
Colony of ants

On Working From Home During Lockdown

Swallows whirl and dance
Cotton clouds in azure sky
Framed by my window

Lawnmowers whirring
Outside my office window
My life in lockdown

I noticed at the beginning of lockdown, when people were "working from home" that there were an awful lot of lawnmowers and raucous group gatherings audible throughout the working day from my home office. When I made this tongue in cheek observation on social media, I very quickly had to leave local groups for fear of an angry mob with pitchforks turning up on my doorstep to lynch me!

This next verse continues the theme.

Hard working from home
Perfectly manicured lawns
Netflix and chilling

Seen From my window
Eucalyptus branches wave
A cold wind stirring

The Perils of Driving

Bright sunny morning
Camera records the scene
Three points on licence

This is a cheery verse, celebrating the glorious sunny morning, taking photographs for posterity until you realise that the camera is actually a traffic camera, catching a speeding motorist. I was misfortunate enough to be caught doing 33 mph in a 30 zone and as a result had to attend a speed awareness course to atone for my sins.

Watching reactions
As a car injures a child
Speed awareness course

At the other extreme are those who think 20 miles over the speed limit is still not enough, and insist on overtaking on blind bends.

In such a hurry
To kill or maim each other
Knobs on country roads

In amongst the trees

Mangled wreckage of a car
Drivers aren't pilots

Whenever there is good weather predicted, and especially if it falls on a public holiday, there is an exodus to the coast to sit elbow to elbow with others on the beach.

A convoy of cars
Beneath sunny azure skies
Heading for the coast

A friend of mine refers to motor cyclists as "organ donors", such is the reckless and carefree way they ride on country roads. Given how exposed they are you would think they might exercise a little more caution and common sense.

On fast country roads
Motor cyclists overtake
As organ donors

They drive like madmen
Morons in expensive cars
On wintery roads

Despite the treacherous road conditions some drivers still insist on driving like lunatics.

White blindness descends
Snowfall obscures everything
Traffic crawls slowly

Cars on icy roads
Where are they all going to
In this new lockdown

During the earliest days of lockdown in the UK people were encouraged to only make necessary journeys. It made me wonder what necessary journeys all these people were actually making, and exactly how necessary they were.

Spring

After the miserable, dark, cold months of winter, the snows thaw and the nature stirs from it's hibernation. As the months progress there is an exuberance of flowers and blossom. It is a new beginning and a return of old friends.

A gentle breeze stirs
A bed of gold and silver
Swaying daffodils

Sweet scent of springtime
Embarrassment of beauty
Apple blossom blush

Bursting rosy buds

Roseaceous red petals
Hawthorn in flower

In my neighbour's garden is a beautiful hawthorn tree. Unusually it has rosy pink double blossom rather than the more common white flowers. By mid spring it is looking magnificent.

Outside my window
Blackbird trilling like a phone
Trolling like a pro

Blackbirds have the ability to mimic sounds, but rarely use it. We have a particular bird who visits the garden and amusingly works through a repertoire of mobile phone tones, trills and sirens. I wonder if the calls will get passed to his offspring.

Summer

As summer rolls by everything becomes much more lazy and lethargic.

Fierce radiant orb
In a cloudless azure blue
Enraptures my soul

Wheeling in blue skies
Dancing with summer's approach
House martins return

Lush grassy meadow
Fronds sway in soft summer breeze
Bug bitten ankles

Rods of cool, fresh rain

A sudden Summer shower
Soon over. Lush green grass

Big blousy flowers
Large white and yellow trumpets
Sway in the warm breeze

Upon stirring sea
Of yellow mustard flowers
The sun sinks westward

Miserable rain
Dark cloud filled skies above me
Shitey Brit Summer

Cerise coloured skies
The sun's last rosy kisses
As daylight recedes

A black butterfly
Fancy phantom flutterer
transiently ghosts by

A haze of blue fog
On a warm summer evening
Smells like sausages

Fluffy little clouds
Swallows darting after flies
Soon will fly southward

Slim blue leaves stirring
In the gentle midday breeze
butterfly flits by

Lovely sunny face
Atop a slender green stalk
Reflects the fierce sun

Proud flower beware!
Beauty amid the grasses

Mower approaches

Afternoon's sun glow
Bathing everything in warmth
Inspires lethargy

Wind stirring the trees
Waving and swaying like limbs
Autumn approaches

Shadows dance on stone
They stir in celebration
Last days of Summer

Pink petals adrift
Float in the water basin
Advancing summer

The flitting flower
Seen defying gravity
Is a butterfly

Withered Christmas wreath
Hanging from the flaking door
Almost four months old

House in sparkling lights
A festive feast to behold
In early August

Amid a jungle
Of fronds I sit and read
A lazy Sunday

Hazy afternoon
Lazily lulled to sleep by
The wood pigeon call

Mowing the garden
In a thirty degree blaze
The haze of summer

The buzz of insects
Delicate flower meadow
Bee rated resort

Birds serenade Strauss
As a warm breeze gently stirs
A flower meadow

Days getting longer
Conceivably explains why
I feel so exhausted

Late in the garden
The blackbird sings his sweet song
To the setting sun

Golden light recedes
As I sit gently reading
Nearby koi are feeding

A radiant glow
Feel the heat kissing your face
The sun's warm embrace

A radiant glow
Feel the heat kissing your face
Goodbye possessions

Autumn

By autumn the leaves of the trees are taking on fierce reds, oranges as yellow. Farmers are bringing in the crops from their fields and migratory birds are beginning their journeys to warmer climes as the evenings are getting darker much earlier. It is time of year rich with imagery for haiku.

> Evening sunlight rays
> Sets fire to glowing leaf
> Gold, amber and green

> Only silence now
> Where once chicks were hatched and raised
> Shit on bay window

Every year we have house martins which nest in the eaves of the houses all around us. All summer they whirl, dip and dive as they search and feed on insects, but by the end of summer they have gone, leaving guano encrusted all over the roof of the bay window.

Gold and rust brown leaves
Hiss like paper in the breeze
Winter approaches

A bronze leaf tumbles
Turns in the golden sunlight
A chill in the air

A bronze leaf tumbles
Turns in the golden sunlight
Autumn's harbinger

Fiery orange glow
Trees in fierce autumn colour
Wind stirs fallen leaves

Sunlight refracted
Glistening diamond dew
A chill in the air

A flaming hillside
Alight with orange, reds and gold
Autumn finery

Rosy orange skies
Greet the slowly dawning day
Autumn's final flush

Leaves crunch under foot
Summer has left the building
Say hello to fall

Autumn's rosy kiss
Leads delicate leaves to blush
Pride before the fall

Pale sun breaking through
Autumnal gold canopy
Cold stillness abounds

Sinking slowly down
Towards the sombre tree line
Early autumn sun

Wheels of golden straw
All lined up across a field
The autumn harvest

House martins have gone
They no longer wheel and dive
The sky is bereft

Sun's rays warm my face
A pause, welcome reprieve from
Autumns march onward

On roadside verges
Resplendent ruby flowers
Blazing red poppies

Natures finest gold
Nestling in the roots of trees
Crisp fallen leaves

Follow the leader
Here's hoping he knows the way
Birds migrating South

Pale sun sinks westward
Autumn's finery now spent
A chill in the air

Rusty brown oak leaves
Rustling like dry paper
Gathered in puddles

Winter

By mid-winter the sun is low in the sky, bathing everything in a pale, yellow light. The air is crisp and there is the hint of snow on the frigid air.

Watery Yellow
Golden sunlight through grey cloud
Reflected on snow

Iron frozen hills
Recede into cold distance
My breath a white cloud

Cold gnaws my fingers
On a frigid winter morn
Ground hard as iron

They snuggle tightly
World sleeps under snow blankets
Winter coldness bites

On a frozen lake
Once the island home to herons
Long deserted now

Celestial light
Bathing in your ghostly glow
Wintery Snow moon

There is something ethereal and unreal about moonlight on snow or
frost. Everything emits a celestial glow.

A silence descends
In large white snowflakes flurries
The world slumbers on

Falling snow dampens sound so everything becomes muffled and
quiet.

Powder petal snow
Falls from cloudless azure skies
Beneath the Rowan

On a woodland walk the skies were crystal clear and cloudless, but
the hoar frost on the tree branches was falling like a powdery snow.

Snuggling warm beneath
A cosy winter blanket
Though heating is on

Bright winter berries
Vivid warm colours amid
The seasonal grey

Pyracantha berries stand out in vivid reds and yellow through the
winter months against the evergreen leaves.

Crisp frozen snowfall

Cracks and crunches underfoot
Red faces, numb hands

There is something quite satisfying about the way the ground freezes in winter, giving you something solid to walk on through fields and woodland that would otherwise be ankle deep in mud. The crunch is also audibly gratifying.

Silent snow falling
Blankets a world in slumber
Coffee warms my hands

It has hidden depths
And can leave a nasty taste
Beware yellow snow

Bust most especially stay away from the brown snow.

Fierce battle rages
Casualties on both side
Wintery snowball fight

Against leaden skies
Boughs festooned with crisp white snow
A lone crow heads home

Through banks of soft snow
Tender grass stems reach for light
Life always persists

White snow laden fields
These hedges march forever on
Whatever weather

On their lofty perch
These sea pigeons warm their feet
"No snow up here mate"

I like the idea that gulls are essentially pigeons of the sea. Sat atop a street light they are well clear of the snow that thickly blankets the ground.

A world turned white
Virgin snows crunch underfoot
A cold north wind blows

Footprints in the snow
Mark the course of busy lives
Not all are human

This was prompted by seeing cat prints in the fresh snows which had fallen in the garden.

The hard icy ground
Cracks and crunches underfoot
Beneath frosted trees

Sunlight weakly probes
Through bare twisted, frosted boughs
Woodland in winter

Glittering diamonds
Sit atop the frozen snow
Frosted ice crystals

A pale sun rises
Yellow light greets the new day
Captured in ice gems

Clear blue skies belie
The bitter cold of Winter
Icy underfoot

Smouldering away
Amid the crisp snowy fields
Steaming pile of sh!t

In a field beside the road was a huge pile of horse manure, gently giving off steam as the microbial action deep within heated up.

Under frosted boughs
Powdery snows still falling

Despite the noon sun

Snow frosted forest
Picture postcard perfection
Winter wonderland

I was amused with the alliteration in this haiku. Does anyone know of a word for snow that starts with "f"?

In the bitter cold
The frost rimed grass so sublime
No-one to see it

Against frozen snows
Yellow gorse shining like gold
Defiant flower

Radiant glory
A splash of vibrant colour
Bright winter berries

If a snow flake falls
In the forest of the night
No one hears it scream

Knowingly nonsensical and perhaps a little disturbing, this is another nod to Zen koans and sayings such as "do bears shit in the woods", "if a tree falls in the woods...", "what is the sound of one hand clapping". If no one is there to witness, how do we know it didn't happen? There is also a hint of the tag line for the film Alien about this one – "In space no-one can hear you scream."

White water rushing
Sluicing, splashing over rock
Memories of snow

Death, Loss and Grief

> Sharing my cold bed
> With the bitter ghost of you
> Through the longest nights

I imagined what it must be like to lose your partner, and how empty and lonely the bed must feel.

> Laid beside his wife
> In a busy hospital
> Even beyond death

Here I am imagining an elderly couple who have been admitted to hospital together with Covid. Sadly neither have made it.

> Even beyond death

Body resting in the ground
The bank gets it's share

After your death, the banks and lawyers will make sure they get their cut first.

Black clad mourners weep
At the solemn graveside
A blackbird singing

At the end of life
What rich stories you could tell
If you were not dead

You will take them with you. Some will remain forever unknown.

In another age
Loving arms would hold you safe
Now just memories

I was remembering being nursed by my mother, the feeling of warmth, love and security. Now long gone.

Lost in silent grief
He stands beside the grave where
Once he was buried

I like that this one turns somewhere quite unexpected on then last line.

Books

I have always been a voracious reader, and will get through over a hundred books a year, on all subjects including fiction and non fiction. I call my pile of tbr (to be read) books "book mountain".

Books on books on books
On top of books on more books
Must stop buying books

Relentlessly on
Page by page ever upwards
I climb book mountain

Pointlessness writ large
Japanese literature
Mountains from molehills

I believe that there is something quite peculiar about the Japanese psyche that causes them to be more generally satisfied with their lot in life, and their place in a somewhat hierarchical society. They have great respect for their elders and superiors and are subject to great social pressure to work hard, contribute to society and to conform. This is reflected in a great deal of their contemporary literature which is often about small or relatively insignificant human dramas. To western sensibilities they might seem a little dull and lack-lustre.

The Hole of Horcum

The Hole of Horcum is a glacial valley formed during the last ice age in the Tabular Hills of the North Yorkshire Moors, with scenic walks and stunning views. Legend has it that the immense Devil's Punchbowl was formed when a giant scooped up a great handful of earth to throw at his wife during an argument.

> Silent shadows scud
> Across a verdant valley
> Occupied by sheep

Irregular clouds scudding across the sun threw dancing shadows across the hills on the other side of the valley as we commenced our walk.

From the carpark we crossed the road and turned left, following the footpath around the brow of the valley, through the gorse and heather. It became increasingly overgrown as we progressed, until we were hacking our way through dense overgrowth like something out of an Indiana Jones movie. It turns out we should have turned right and followed the clearly marked footpath...

Bracken surrounds me
A half-imagined footpath
This Hell of Horcum

Horcum water falls
A steaming stream of yellow
from a cow's behind

There were no cascading waterfalls, only those that occurred when a cow chose to let flow great gushing gallons of urine.

Lakes

The image is view across one of the many lakes in the Lake District in Cumbria.

White water cascades
Foams and tumbles over stone
Catching golden sun

A view from a hill
Wind stirred lake surface
Shimmering sunlight

Ponds

The father of haiku, Matsuo Basho, wrote a famous haiku that, translated into English, reads something as follows: *an old pond / a frog jumps in / plop!* The following two verses were my tribute to this classic haiku.

Serene old pond
A fish leaps out
Plop! Ripples recede

A silent old pond
A weighted body thrown in
Silence. Might be best

In this tongue in cheek version the silence is disturbed by a human corpse being disposed of, presumably by criminals. The implied threat is that if you don't keep quiet, you will be next.

Graceful grey heron
Perched regally, high above
Eyes my precious koi

During my first week working from home due to Covid lockdown I was eating breakfast by the window when I saw a huge pterodactyl like bird circling the house. I rushed out to the garden to see a heron sat on my roof eyeing my koi pond. Had I been working from the office I would likely have come home to an empty pond. Needless to say, it was very quickly covered with a raised net to protect the fish from future visits.

Yellow eye in pond
Floats amid green lily pads
Then too soon is gone

Through duck weed peering
On balmy summer evening
Tiny frog bathing

Amid lily pads
Red, white and yellow fish feed.
A bird sings proudly

Excuse me I see
Your pond filled with rock and plants
Hard water issues?

A friend and former work colleague posted a picture of work done in her garden, and what looked like a great opportunity for a raised pond had been filled with earth and gravel for a flowerbed.

In a dense reed bed
A heron sits patiently
Death does not hurry

Rain falls on a pond
As carp glide slowly by
Nice weather for ducks

Circles in circles
Within circles in a square
Rainfall on the pond

I liked the imagery created by geometric shapes within shapes of this verse, with the idea of raindrops forming circular ripples on the surface of the pond.

Like swift silver darts
And elegant wafting fans
I watch my koi swim

Better than tv
Watching koi roll, splash and play
Earthly paradise

Playful splash and roll
A fishy feeding frenzy
The sun falls westward

Black fleeting vision
Life in fear amongst the weeds
A baby goldfish

Although starting out with ten koi and five goldfish, I have now lost count as the goldfish keep spawning and we occasionally see tiny black "mystery fish" darting in and out of the reeds.

"No more fish" he said
"The pond overstocked," he said
"Hello my pretties!"

So now I agonise and worry that we may have too many fish for the size of pond…

Dawn chorus in dark
The moon dances on the pond
Beneath the cascade

The following marks a repeat visit from the heron. As I was filling making myself a warm drink, I looked up to see him sat on the garden fence directly above the pond. They are graceful birds, but voracious predators that I do not want near my pond. Fortunately it is now protected by a raised net.

Preparing coffee
Hands in hot soapy water
Heron watching koi

Amongst the reed beds
The only thing twitching
Is my restless legs

I composed this on a visit to a local nature reserve. I liked the duality of twitching relating both to bird watching or muscle spasms.

Old Photographs

> Gazing at us from
> The near dim and distant past -
> Ghosts, old photographs

This feels like a particularly personal and poignant haiku verse to me, especially so when paired with the image which shows family members – parents, grandparents, aunts and uncles – all now long gone.

The following verse has similar sentiments, though was about unknown faces in formal poses from the turn of the last century.

> Moments caught in time
> We will never see their like
> Faces in photos

Regarding the Crane Fly

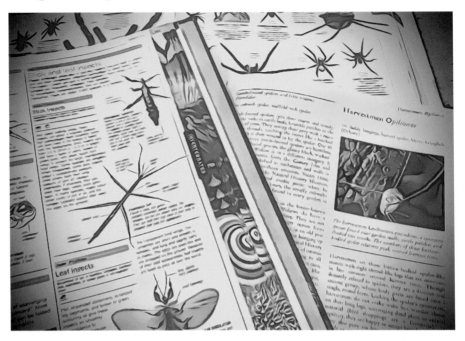

For years it has annoyed me that people refer to winged "crane flies" (of the family Tipulidae) as "daddy long legs", when clearly daddy long legs are a particular species of spider (Pholcus phalangioides) with tiny round bodies and wiry, long legs.

> This is no spider
> Paternal or otherwise
> This leggy crane fly

> No daddy long legs
> Identity confusion
> This is a crane fly

A quick trawl of Google showed that in fact both are correct, shooting my argument down in flames. I will crawl back under my rock.

Fast Food

A lunch on the go
Is only convenience food
If you can catch it

I love sushi, and very much enjoy the experience of eating at Yo! Sushi with it's fun conveyor belts of domed sushi dishes trundling by. You need to be quick though, or it's gone before you can grab it...

On Unidentified Flying Objects

Leading up to the millennium I was a regular reader of UFO Magazine, and together with a friend and work colleague Paul Stephen, attendee at the annual UFO Conference hosted in Leeds. Paul and I had bonded as friends at work over our love of the weird and supernatural. The conferences drew experts and experiencers of the subject from all around the world to give speeches, show videos and to answer questions.

It was always an intensely interesting experience, as much for the people watching as it was for the tales of pilot encounters, flying saucers and alien abductions. I was always one of the more grounded, rational people there. For me a highlight each year were the talks given by local Russel Callaghan, an unassuming, soft spoken gentleman, who often skillfully dismantled whatever had been the previous year's big piece of footage or world class evidence by process of logical deduction and example. Often he had photos or examples of models which might have been used to fake video footage and photos.

At a time of increasing pre-millennial tension, and with television shows like the X-Files at their height, and intense popularity of New Age thinking it was oft repeated that world governments were preparing for an imminent public disclosure of the reality of alien contact. Well, the millennium came and went, and life continued as normal, without E.T. revealing himself. Sadly Graham Birdsall, author of UFO Magazine, died of a cerebral hemorrhage in 2003 and was a great loss to the UFO community..

With hindsight much of what people were seeing or experiencing was a combination of self-delusion, wishful thinking and misidentified military drones or Chinese lanterns. Since the demise of UFO Magazine the UK based UFO community has largely disappeared.

These haiku verses came as a result of remembering these times and experiences shared.

Unknown flying craft
As flown by little grey men
Probably Russian

Strange lights in the sky
Forms not from around this way
Probably marsh gas

Project Blue Book was the code name for a systematic study of unidentified flying objects carried out by the United States Air Force between 1952 and 1959. Considered an official white wash and cover up by many, several sightings were dismissed as "marsh gas".

Wreckage at Roswell
What a load of dummies
Weather balloon crash

The famed Roswell incident involved the recovery of unidentified debris from a farmer's ranch in New Mexico in July, 1947. After an initial press release where the air force claimed they had recovered a crashed disk, the story was quickly retracted. Renowned nuclear scientist and UFO investigator Stanton Friedman spent years interviewing military and civilian personnel who claimed to have had involvement in recovering a crashed alien spacecraft and alien bodies. The details are covered his book **Crash at Corona**. Friedman died in 2019 at the age of 89. The final Roswell Report: Case Closed official review released in 1997 concluded that the bodies seen had been misidentified "crash test dummies".

Lamenting A Cruise Holiday

Before the Corona virus struck, we had booked to sail around the Canary Islands on a luxury cruise during September 2020. With the virus raging, and early horror stories about stranded cruise ship passengers being refused permission to dock, the last place we wanted to be at the time was onboard a floating petri dish, no matter how pampered.

Canaries can wait
Patience being a virtue
In pandemic times

Places we didn't see
Memories we didn't make
Lamenting a cruise

City on the sea

Memories we didn't share
We will meet again

These following verses are reminiscent of an old fashioned, hand written postcard sent home from some exotic location, and reporting the weather to disinterested family.

Today not sailing
Across the Bay of Biscay
Weather terrible

Week two not sailing
Round the Canary Islands
Weather picking up

Covid 19

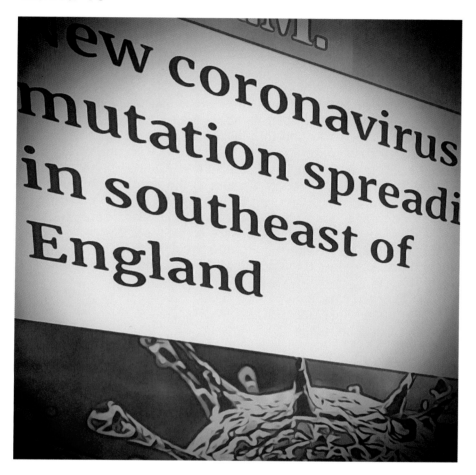

The United Kingdom first went into lockdown to fight the spread of the COVID virus in late March 2020. Just before that happened selfish shoppers had started panic buying and putting great strain on the supermarket supply chains with their abnormal demand for common domestic products such as toilet rolls, bread and pasta. Despite calls for calm, a "me first" mentality set in with some shoppers. On one occasion I witnessed an elderly gentleman with crate of UHT loaded into his shopping trolley – 48 litres of long-life milk. It was infuriating that such levels of inconsiderate behaviour, greed and selfishness meant that other would have to go without whilst others had unnecessary stockpiles to last 12 months. If only sanity and level heads would prevail then the end of civilization and collapse of social order would be averted.

It defies logic
Trolley loads of toilet roll
COVID Panic buy

Under lockdown unnecessary travel was discouraged with police stopping and questioning people about their journeys. Only a week after the country had gone into lockdown Dominic Cummings had made a 264 mile round trip with his infected wife and child to his parent in Durham, famously visiting Barnard Castle on the way. The scandal caused great embarrassment to the Johnson government, to which Cummings was a senior advisor. The unrepentant Cummings made some feeble excuse about child care and bad eyesight. Many, including myself, were so incensed by the hypocrisy on display that they furiously wrote to their MPs. Others claimed it would cause damage to the public will to obey the lockdown rules.

In Barnard Castle
For an eye test? Cannot see
Dominic Cummings

At the end of the initial lockdown coffee shops and restaurants finally opened but with restrictions on numbers and facemasks were required indoors. Everyone was required to scan a QR code for purposes of track and trace in the event of infection.

You cannot sit there
An abundance of caution
Much thanks to covid

Scan this QR code
Before you can come inside
Luddites are exempt

The Luddites were the technophobes who smashed up machinery in the woolen mills in the 1800s. Here I am referring to a generation perhaps less familiar with mobile phones who struggled with scanning QR codes.

Masks worn everywhere
Obsessive washing of hands
COVID damn panic

Here, in the last line the phrase "damn panic" is a play on the word pandemic.

The prevalence of the virus as it spread across the country gave rise to fear and suspicion. Since anyone might have it, but be asymptomatic, even the least little sniffle or cough was cause for alarm.

This dry cough of mine
Is nothing so serious
No need to panic

Your palpable fear
There's no need to back away
I only coughed

Depression descends
Future becomes uncertain
Covid surges back

Restless, sleepless nights
How it interrupts my dreams
This COVID nightmare

There were reports that due to the disruption and anxiety caused in people's lives due to lockdowns that many were experiencing disturbed sleep or vivid dreams.

It's not for ever
It's just for now. Mask, wash, space
COVID precautions

It is no great sacrifice to wear a mask, wash hands or keep a little distance. The virus is spreading through human contact, and is making some people critically ill. It's not a lot to ask, and it's not forever.

Lateral flow test
For the COVID infection
Was made in China

Here I am playing on the idea that many seek to blame China for the virus. I note ironically that the test kits, part of the solution, are of Chinese manufacture. There is some intentional ambiguity in the verse. Am I saying that the test kit is of Chinese origin, or the virus? In truth, once it had started spreading it didn't matter where it originated, only what people were going to do to mitigate it's effect. It's a bit like looking for who struck the match while your house is burning to the ground.

Society sleeps
Isolates and hibernates
Better times will come

When it's all over
Amongst the memories this:
Discarded face masks

In this age of video on demand, and binge watched box sets I imagined the COVID 19 situation as a television drama series. As the current season draws to a close in 2020 with the virus coming under control, everyone is looking forward to easing restrictions and returning to a life under the "new normal". Then suddenly we are sideswiped by an unexpected twist in the season finale, as the virus mutates into a more virulent strain and infections again soar. What will happen now? Tune in next season to find out…

Season finale
A deadly new strain emerges
Covid mutated

Christmas

This covid season
Exuberant Christmas cheer
Stick it up your arse

With the general sense of gloom over the COVID lockdown there was palpable lack of Christmas spirit. The shops had been closed for months, with people doing any gift shopping online, and the scientists were issuing dire warnings to avoid family gatherings for fear of killing granny with kindness and COVID 19.

> Air of reverence
> Tranquility created
> By soft candle light

> Snow blanketed world
> Christmas card perfect image
> Sheep seem unimpressed

> Praying to Santa
> These dyslexic Satanists
> Though neither exist

I was amused by the idea that Santa and Satan might cause confusion to someone challenged by dyslexia. I hope I'm not breaking any disappointing news or childhood illusions here.

> Festive carols sung
> Crackling log in the fireplace
> Christmas screen saver

> A brass band plays
> Caught on security cam
> Christmas cheer abounds

This might be imagined to relate to footage captured on a security camera in a shopping mall. In fact it relates to one of my neighbours who was seriously ill with a degenerative condition. A brass band had been booked to play Christmas carols for what may well be his last Christmas. Hold your loved ones close and celebrate good times with them. You never know when it will be your last opportunity.

> A warm orange glow
> Cast across grey cloud blankets
> Christmas Eve sunrise

> Faint sound of sleigh bells
> Heavy footsteps on the roof

Children slumber on

Muddy footprint trail
All about the unlit fire
Not Santa, but cats

A gentle pink blush
Spreads across a winter sky
Merry Christmas all

New Year

Year-end approaches
Pleased to see the back of
This pandemic year

New Year approaches
All hope it is better than
This pandemic year

Wishing you were here
You cannot come soon enough
Twenty twenty-one

Written wistfully in December 2020, it turned out that 2021 was set to be a rerun of 2020.

Afterword

Thank you for taking the time and trouble to read this book.

It is my sincere hope that you found heart, wisdom and wit between these pages, that you were moved to tears or laughter.

I hope that it imparted on you some small fraction of the joy and pleasure it brought me to compose the verses and put together the work you hold in your hands.

If any of the haiku or images resonated with you then I would be humbled and grateful if you might take the time to give a review on Amazon or Goodreads.

Again, thank you for indulging me.

Bibliography and Further Reading

Adams, Douglas. **The Hitchhiker's Guide to the Galaxy**. Pan Books. 1979

Aitken, Robert. **The River of Heaven. The Haiku of Basho, Buson, Issa and Shiki**. Counterpoint. 2011

Basho, Matsuo. **Lips Too Chilled**. Penguin Books. 1985

Basho, Matsuo. **On Love and Barley – Haiku of Basho**, Penguin Books. 1985

Basho, Matsuo. **The Narrow Road to the Deep North and Other Travel Sketches**. Penguin Books. 1966

Bowers, Faubion. **The Classic Tradition of Haiku. An Anthology**. Dover Thrift Editions. 1996

Bowring, Richard (translator). **The Diary of Lady Murakami**. Penguin Books. 1996

Cobb, David. **The British Museum Haiku.** The British Museum Press. 2002

Doughty, Bill. **Haiku of Trump: The Chasm, Schism & Isms of Donald J. Trump**. 2020

Friedman, Stanton T. **Crash at Corona**. Paragon House.1992

Herbert, Frank. **Dune**. Chilton Books. 1965

Higginson, William J and Penny Harter: **Haiku Handbook**. Kodansha USA Publishing LLC, 2013

Kenko and Chomei. **Essays in Idleness and Hojoki**. Penguin Books. 2013

Kenko, Yoshida. **A Cup of sake Beneath the Cherry Trees**. Penguin Books

Kern, Adam L. **The Penguin Book of Haiku**. Penguin Books. 2018
King, Stephen. **The Tommyknockers**. Putnam. 1987

Kodama, Misao & Yanagishima, Hikosaku, **The Zen Fool Ryokan**. Tuttle. 1999

Lanoue, David G. **Pure Land Haiku: The Art of Priest Issa**. Buddhist Books International. 2013

Lanoue, David G. **Write Like Issa: A Haiku How-To**. 2017

Lindley, David. **How to Write Haiku**. Verborum Editions. 2016

Lowenstein, Tom. **Classic Haiku**. Shelter Harbor Press. 2007

MacMillan, Peter (translator). **One Hundred Poets, One Poem Each**. Penguin Books. 2018

McKinney, Meredith (translator). **Travels With a Writing Brush. Classical Japanese Travel Writing From Manyoshu to Basho**, Penguin Books. 2019

Morris, Desmond. **Catwatching, The Essential Guide to Cat Behaviour**. Ebury Press. 2002

Oyama, Sumita. **The Life and Zen Haiku Poetry of Santoka Taneda**. Tuttle Publishing. 2021

Patt, Judith, Warkentype, Michiko and Till, Barry. **Haiku. Japanese Art and Poetry**. Pomegranate Communications Inc. 2010

Pilbeam, Mavis. **The British Museum Haiku Animals**. The British Museum Press. 2010

Smith, Lester. **Cthulhu Haiku and Other Mythos Madness**. Popcorn Press. 2012

Tudge, Colin. **The Secret Life of Trees**. Penguin Books. 2005

Tyler, Dominick. **Uncommon Ground. A word-lover's guide to the British landscape**. Guardian Books. 2015

Nordström, Ulrica. **Moss: from forest to garden : a guide to the hidden world of moss**. Michael Joseph. 2019

Washington, Peter. **Haiku**. Everyman's Library Pocket Poets. 2003

About the Author

Jason Hanrahan lives in Yorkshire, UK, with his partner, two cats and an indeterminate number of koi. He is a software developer with twenty-five years experience and has worked on projects for a host of household names. In his spare time, he cultivates bonsai, loves cinema, and reads Eastern philosophy and literature.

This is his first haiku collection.

Printed in Poland
by Amazon Fulfillment
Poland Sp. z o.o., Wrocław
24 November 2021

c8fe7801-2c52-4ee6-ac5b-c87ca9430d78R15